The Ministry of Administrative Assistants

Abingdon Press & The Church of the Resurrection
Ministry Guides

The Ministry of Administrative Assistants

Sue Thompson

Adam Hamilton, Series Editor

ABINGDON PRESS
Nashville

THE MINISTRY OF ADMINISTRATIVE ASSISTANTS

Copyright © 2008 by Abingdon Press

This book is printed on acid-free paper.

Library of Congress Cataloging-in-Publication Data

Thompson, Sue.
    The ministry of administrative assistants / Sue Thompson.
       p. cm. — (The Abingdon Church of the Resurrection ministry guides ; 7)
    Includes bibliographical references.
    ISBN 978-0-687-64709-5 (binding: pbk., adhesive binding : alk. paper)
    1. Church secretaries. 2. Administrative assistants. I. Title.
    BV705.T46 2008
    254—dc22

                                                                    2008017344

08 09 10 11 12 13 14 15 16 17—10 9 8 7 6 5 4 3 2 1
MANUFACTURED IN THE UNITED STATES OF AMERICA

Contents

Foreword

....

Behind any successful venture are those people who are gifted at turning ideas into action. They look at a goal and immediately see the series of steps that must be taken to achieve it. They help all the diverse players work together to accomplish the goals. They manage and pursue the day-to-day details with aplomb. And they have a knack for organizing chaos and "herding cats." They are often unsung heroes and heroines.

They go by different names, but in this book they're referred to as "administrative assistants." This position, whether held by a paid staff member or a volunteer, is as important to the ministry of the church as that of the pastor or any other leader.

For more than a decade now, Sue Thompson has served as my executive administrative assistant. I often tell others that I work for Sue. She manages my time, keeps my calendar and helps organize the chaos of my life and ministry. She ministers to thousands of people each year directly through her phone presence, her e-mail, and her care for persons, both staff and laity, who come into our office. She offers valuable insights to me, assists in research and she handles the details of virtually everything that I do. Her work has played a key role in the growth and development of our church and in every dimension of my ministry.

....

At The Church of the Resurrection, we live daily with the goal to help people become deeply committed Christians. More than nominally religious. More than the Sunday pew holder. More than the spectator. We know these same people become more by doing more. We begin with the knowledge that people want the church to be theirs. They want to know God has a place for them. With that in mind, we recognized from the very start that specialized ministries utilizing the skills and talents of laypeople are fundamental to church life. A church on the move will have specialized ministries capitalizing on the skills and talents of laypeople. They are your keys to succeed.

In developing these guides, we listened to the requests of smaller churches for practical resources to enlist laypeople for this purpose. These economical guides, written by proven leaders at our church, will serve as essential resources for innovative, creative, and, more than likely, nontraditional church workers who have little or no budget to work with. With these guides in hand, your laypeople will be ready to plunge into the work with excitement and courage instead of tentatively approaching it on tiptoe. At the core of these guides is the belief that anything is possible. It's a challenge, but it's a truth. God can and does use us all—with that conviction we bring hope to the world.

—Adam Hamilton
Senior Pastor
The Church of the Resurrection
Leawood, Kansas

Introduction

We're changing. The office of yesterday is no more, and sometimes it's a scramble just to keep up. When I was asked to write this ministry guide, my first thought was how I could give information to help those in support ministry to do more than just keep up. While writing directly for the administrative assistant, I wanted the guide to prove helpful for pastors, parish committees in charge of selecting church employees, and even for the volunteer who works several hours a week.

I work for a senior pastor, so in this guide I will always refer to the pastor; however, I've included the information for those who may work for an associate pastor, ministry director or coordinator, or a leadership team, or for those who may work as church receptionists with support responsibilities.

This guide is also for people who work in many different ministry settings, both large and small churches, a church or denominational administrative office, a parachurch (Christian business nonprofits or organizations that work across denominations to accomplish ministry and associations that provide ministry) or a missions-focused organization.

My prayer for this ministry guide is that anyone who provides support will take away something that will assist him or her in looking at ministry and the level of support that is needed for a particular setting. I hope as you look at some of these ideas that they will spark for you something that could be done differently or more efficiently in your office—I encourage you to take these ideas and mold and change them to fit your particular work and ministry situation.

When I say *your particular work and ministry situation*, I want to stress this as a key concept. With a position as administrative assistant, you will bring particular skills to the job. But, where you work in particular will make a difference in how you are able to actually *do* your job. My situation won't be the same as yours, but key elements that an administrative assistant performs will be the same, such as:

Calendar management
Correspondence/Communications
Information Management

The components of your job will be identified where you work. (See page 51 for a job description.) Your job also may include:

Meeting and event organization
Making travel arrangements
Budgeting
Participating in meetings
Project/team coordination
Project management
Designing presentations
Taking minutes
Research
Coaching/training others

Writing reports
New initiatives

Sometimes you may find in your job that you are asked to do something outside your comfort zone. For example, I never thought of writing a book—but here it is!

While I've included easy tips, valuable timesavers, and ideas to implement—and concentrate a great deal on the position itself—I want to stress maybe the most important part of your job: to pray for the pastor daily. As the administrative assistant, you are the staff member who knows what is on your pastor's agenda on any given day. There will be challenges, routine work, surprises, blessings, and frustrations that will cross the pastor's path. Pray for the pastor each morning; ask God how you can be a blessing as the pastor goes about the ministry he or she has been called to. Pray that your partnership in this ministry will be a blessing to your coworkers and your congregation.

CHAPTER ONE

The Ministry of Administration

NOW YOU ARE THE BODY OF CHRIST, AND EACH ONE OF
YOU IS A PART OF IT. AND IN THE CHURCH GOD HAS
APPOINTED FIRST OF ALL APOSTLES, SECOND PROPHETS, THIRD
TEACHERS, THEN WORKERS OF MIRACLES, ALSO THOSE HAVING
GIFTS OF HEALING, THOSE ABLE TO HELP OTHERS, THOSE WITH
GIFTS OF ADMINISTRATION, AND THOSE SPEAKING IN DIFFERENT
KINDS OF TONGUES. —I CORINTHIANS 12:27-28 (NIV)

More than ten years ago I was about to re-enter the work-force; I was attending a local community college and was near completion of a professional certificate in paralegal studies. One Sunday the attendance notebooks were being passed in church, and I noticed an ad on the front page that indicated The Church of the Resurrection was looking for an administrative assistant for the senior pastor. I was drawn to the ad with some interest, even though it wasn't paralegal work.

I had no formal administrative support experience, but I did have a long list of volunteer experiences that demon-strated my abilities to organize things and people, manage projects, maintain a schedule, communicate by phone and letter (e-mail was not as prevalent at that time), maintain files, and all of those other tasks it takes to support a person in a business office. Also on my resume was the information about different church projects and mission trips in which I had participated.

The initial interview went well, and I was asked back to interview with the senior pastor and two members of the staff parish committee who were interviewing eight candidates. Not much later I received a phone call from the senior pastor extending an invitation for me to join the staff at The Church of the Resurrection as his administrative assistant. I had wanted to be a paralegal, not someone's assistant, but I felt a strong prompting to accept this position.

From this I would advise that it's important when you are interviewing for a support position in a church or ministry setting to go through a discernment process to aid you in making a decision. Time in prayer, a closer look at the job description, and a good understanding of the church organization can help you in making your decision. And don't ever be surprised at where God leads you.

A Job Versus a Calling

A call to ministry is an important thing to understand for an administrative assistant; your heart and the way you deal with people and tasks are different if you understand your position as a call to ministry rather than a job for a paycheck. If you understand that you represent not just your pastor and your church but Christ to every person who calls, stops by, e-mails, and so forth, you approach tasks and people differently. Working as the assistant to a pastor, or any person in ministry, you have to approach your tasks with an understanding of whom you are serving—and you are serving Christ and his people. You need to be able to discern the concern or pain in someone's voice as you talk on the phone.

You need to listen and graciously direct callers and guests to the proper person or ministry that can meet their need. You will welcome first-time visitors, potential donors, and people in need. For the people who call or stop by your office, you are the face of your pastor and your church. You need to be able to look at what needs to be done and take the proper action and not wait to be told. You need to understand the impact on the different ministries of the church of any task you undertake. You need to understand how what you do will free up the person you assist to truly focus on the ministry to which he or she is called. This is much more than a job for a paycheck—it is a ministry.

Spiritual Gifts

The role of an administrative assistant has evolved from what used to be the role of a secretary—answering phones, greeting people who came to the office, perhaps managing the boss's calendar, and assembling the church newsletter. Over time and with the development of technology, the role of a secretary has become more of a middle management role. The *assistant* manages projects, makes decisions, and helps control the flow of work and deadlines. In a church this role has become an integral part of the overall ministry, working to manage information and free up pastors to provide leadership and do the hands-on work of the ministry.

MAKE TIME
FOR THIS

Being an assistant, particularly in ministry, is a challenging position and to be successful the person needs to have a good understanding of the position and how individual gifts can enhance it. This will help the administrative assistant feel successful and fulfilled and ultimately help the ministries of the church flourish. I encourage people who want to serve as an assistant to take a spiritual gifts class and assessment. A good spiritual gifts tool will help you assess your strengths. (See Carol

Cartmill and Yvonne Gentile, *Serving from the Heart* [(Nashville: Abingdon Press, 2003]). As part of your discernment process, reflect on your life:

• What activities and interests have brought you the most joy and fulfillment?
• Do you enjoy serving, being the member of the team who organizes the details and assists people with the resources they need?
• Do you have strong gifts in the areas of administration and help?

The Ministry of Being an Assistant

The position of administrative assistant is a vital part of the overall ministry of your church and the congregation. You are the gatekeeper, bridge-builder, keeper of the "information," soother of wounded feelings, and deliverer of unwanted news. You are the person who has your finger on the pulse of your congregation and your community. You are the person people will come to for answers. You will handle thousands of details related to dozens of different projects and commitments for your pastor. You will help make the pastor's ministry seamless.

While all of these things may make your head spin, this is a good description of the ministry of being an assistant. If you understand your job as a ministry and understand your call to this ministry, you will find an interesting position and look forward to going to work each and every day.

And, knowing that your position of administrative assistant is a ministry, you will each day feel the importance of beginning the day with a prayer for wisdom and strength, surrendering your mind and will to God, and preparing yourself to work with the heart of a servant.

Being an administrative assistant isn't for every-one. You need to recognize that being an assistant is a "behind-the-scenes" support role. If you are a person who craves being the "out-front" ministry person, this may not be the role for you. Instead, as an administrative assistant, recognize that your work is what helps make possible the ministries that will impact the lives of your congregation. And often that work includes being not quite as visible as other ministries.

As Christ walks alongside you in your daily life, you will learn to walk alongside the pastor and be an indispensable partner in ministry.

CHAPTER TWO

Partners in Ministry

My first day on the job I was handed a job description that had three items on it. I still have this job description and look at it occasionally to remind myself of where Adam and I started. As I was handed my three-line job description Adam said, "We will have to make this up as we go along." The partnership we built has been a process over the past several years and continues to develop today.

Developing this partnership took a great deal of study and observation on my part. I not only had to learn the details of the position but I also had to learn the Big Picture. What did my boss (I'll say "boss" because this idea is important no matter whom you work for) consider his role to be in the Purpose and Mission of our church? What were his priorities in working toward our goals? How could I assist my boss in meeting his priorities?

Whether you are new to your position as an assistant or looking to take your role to the next level there are really just three simple steps to begin the building of a partnership.

Observe, Listen, and Ask

Three important concepts that are so important—especially when first beginning—are observing, listening, and asking.

1. Observe

I had been attending the Church of the Resurrection for only two months when I applied for the position of the senior pastor's assistant. I had no history with this church and did not know the senior pastor. I soon learned that the purpose statement was the driving force of the church.

▷ **Learn** how the purpose and mission drive the ministries and programs in your church. How do these help your pastor and coworkers set their priorities regarding their tasks?

▷ **Observe** how the ministries relate to one another and work together. Learn what your pastor's role is in setting policy and making decisions. Is your pastor involved in the day-to-day decisions or is that the responsibility of each director?

▷ **See** the work culture in your church. Is it laid back? Full-steam ahead? Get things done early? Does the pressure of the deadline give everyone a rush? You will find that to some extent all of these work styles will exist in your church, and you will need to learn how to balance them.

▷ **Know** the pastor's priorities. Knowing the priorities is important for everything you do in your office.

▷ **Free up** the routine tasks the pastor is doing. In my first twelve months as Adam's administrative assistant I looked for things that I could take off his plate in order for him to concentrate on other projects. As he learned my strengths and gifts, he became more comfortable turning many tasks over to me.

2. Listen

Assistants need to be doers—people who carry out the decision and make things happen. But we can't be so busy doing that we don't take time to listen. In beginning this job

I learned that I had to stop from time to time and just listen. People do not always articulate exactly what their expectations are or what they want you to do. There are times we hear a request, but don't really listen to what is being asked. This is when mistakes or missteps will occur.

3. Ask

When you are beginning as someone's assistant it is very important to ask questions—a lot of questions. If you are not clear on the big picture or details, it is important to ask for clarification. Do not be afraid to ask the *why* questions. Understanding why your church does things a certain way can go a long way in getting you on track with the culture and the day-to-day operations. As you begin your role as the assistant, give yourself five days of observation and listening; carry a notebook with you during this time and write down all those things you don't understand or need to have clarified, and then put yourself on your pastor's schedule toward the end of that time to talk about those things you need to understand better. This will go a long way in helping you on those initial steps of building a partnership with the pastor.

The Assistant's Part in Building an Effective Partnership

The administrative assistant helps take over many of the daily tasks that can sap the pastor's time. That being said, there are other items that are critical to having an effective partnership.

Support the pastor

The pastor needs to know that you are supportive in the work of the ministry. Nothing will undermine a ministry or church more quickly than an assistant who publicly disagrees with the pastor. If you have concerns or thoughts about something your pastor is working on, talk with him or her about it, face-to-face. Express your concerns and thoughts and listen carefully to explanations. In our ministry setting, we call this pushing back. There will be times our executive team or perhaps just the pastor and I will have a discussion on a new ministry or a particular challenge we are facing and at times there is disagreement. Through respectful push-back we are able to get different ideas and perspectives on the table. This is a healthy process. But, when you leave the room, it is important that you support your pastor to the staff, congregation, and community.

Maintain confidentiality

This goes hand-in-hand with supporting your pastor. You will deal with and have knowledge of a lot of very sensitive information, such as confidential communication from congregation members, business dealings of your church, staffing issues, and so on. It is critical to your role as a ministry partner to maintain confidences. Speaking about confidential matters to others is the quickest way for people to lose trust in you. Without trust you cannot be effective in your ministry.

POTENTIAL PITFALL

A note of caution is necessary here. Pastors are bound ethically and protected legally—to a certain extent—in keeping the confidences of those people to whom they provide counseling. There are laws governing counseling sessions that include such things as child abuse, crimes, and so forth, which vary from state to state. If your church doesn't have these in written form, you should make sure this is done. It's in the church's best interest that the administrative assistant know exactly what would need to be reported to authorities.

So, if the pastor wants the administrative assistant to get information when people phone in for appointments, the assistant should first inform callers that if it's a life-threatening emergency, they should call 911. For other crises, the administrative assistant should ask for only basic information that can be communicated to the pastor to help him or her be prepared for a meeting. The administrative assistant can assure the caller that this basic information to be given to the pastor will be kept confidential (if within the bounds of the above laws).

When pastors know they can trust administrative assistants to not share confidential information with others, they will support them in their efforts with both the staff and the congregation. As the pastor reinforces the administrative assistant's role in ministry, people will know this person is a trusted partner in the pastor's ministry.

And, do remember it's important to live in such a way that people know you will not share their confidences or the confidences of your church in inappropriate ways. Do not gossip about your coworkers or congregation members with anyone.

Because you are the pastor's assistant, you may find people confiding many things to you and using you as a sounding board. At times people come to me to vent; sometimes they ask me not to share our conversation with Adam. Here is my rule: if someone tells me something that has the potential of having an effect on Adam or his ministry or our church, I tell him. I tell people that they should not share anything with me that they don't want me to share with Adam; this way people are clear on what is going to happen before they speak.

All of this does not mean that you should not have a safe and confidential place to talk. Working with people in crisis, always facing tight deadlines, and working for someone who is always in demand can be very stressful. It is important that you have a safe and confidential place to unburden your stress. Your circle of friends and supports must be a group that will hold you accountable and keep your confidences. Because I work for my pastor, I try not to share frustrations with my spouse or children. It is important to not taint your family's relationship with the church and their pastor. Instead I have a very small and close-knit group of friends who also serve on staff at The Church of the Resurrection—this is my safe group. We are in covenant relationship with each other and are there for each other to help relieve the stresses and tensions that go along with our ministries. We hold each other accountable for how we handle our stress and self-care.

Have a clear understanding of priorities at all times

Your pastor's time is a resource of your church. It is a resource in the same way as your building, your budget, and other tools of ministry. The time needs to be carefully allocated to all the tasks that help your pastor accomplish his or her goals. In order to allocate the pastor's time you must always have a clear understanding of priorities.

Each year, at review time, Adam will share with me what his goals are for the coming year. Through conversation I get an idea of how those goals are to be weighted and how I should help allocate his time. Adam preaches forty out of fifty-two weeks, so sermon writing is the top priority most weeks. He estimates that it will take him between fifteen and twenty hours per week to prepare his sermon—that is time praying, reading, researching, deciding what resources he will need, and writing several drafts of his sermon. I book that time on his schedule, and I do not schedule anything else during sermon preparation time.

That leaves the rest of his workweek, twenty to thirty hours, for his other priorities.

Priorities constantly change, so it is important to stay on top of what is happening in any given week and make adjustments accordingly. If Adam is going to officiate at a funeral, the priorities for the next few days will shift to allow for funeral preparations, time to meet with the family, put the service together, write the homily for the service, and so on.

Learn the pastor's work style

To be an effective partner, you must have an understanding of work styles. When is the most productive time of day for the pastor? How does the pastor like to receive information? How does he or she feel about interruptions? How are offices to be maintained? How should deadlines be handled? Learning the pastor's work style will help you know how to handle the flow of information that will come across your desk and how to communicate that information to the pastor.

Sometimes what seems like a little thing actually can be a time-saver and a tremendous help. For example, Adam is a voracious note taker; it helps him remember things if he writes them down as he hears them. His method of note taking is on legal pads. I make sure I always have a large supply of legal pads in our office and I keep his desk stocked with them. Because he will take notes at different meetings on one note pad I will sort through them and place the handwritten notes in the appropriate file folders.

Another example has to do with the relational aspect of Adam's ministry. If he is having a meeting with someone, he wants to be able to ask about family, work, or ministry. When he meets with a congregation member I make sure he has the names of the person's immediate family members, ages of children, place of employment, or information about a civic or community organization with whom this person may be working. If there is a health or personal issue I am aware of, I will provide that information also.

Be the complement to the pastor's gifts

The old saying "opposites attract" really applies to the role of a pastor and an administrative assistant. This is a relationship where the two people need to have complementing gifts. If the pastor has a "fluid" relationship with time and has a hard time sticking to a schedule, it would be a train wreck to have an administrative assistant who couldn't maintain a schedule.

In thinking about the pastor's gifts it is critical that the assistant have a clear understanding of his or her own gifts and the ability to look at those strengths to complement the pastor. This is learning to work in harmony to develop creative solutions to challenges—the ability for each to fill in the gaps for the other.

As an example, in our office, Adam is a Big Picture person—he is the visionary leader. I am the detail person. Adam will lay out what he wants done or where he wants to go with a certain project—the part that he doesn't like is the detail involved in how something will get accomplished. That is where I step in with the details regarding time, budget, and other resources.

Eyes, ears, and memory

Working with a pastor, particularly a senior pastor, requires dealing with thousands of details, details a busy pastor probably will not remember. The administrative assistant must be able to look at different projects across many different ministry areas and watch for how things are being carried out and ensure that all the t's are crossed and the i's dotted.

You will need to listen carefully to people and let the pastor know about those things that are of interest. Keep the pastor updated about different things happening in the lives of staff and congregation members. Yes, staff too. For example, not long ago I had a phone conversation with one of our ministry directors and learned that one of his children was having surgery. He had notified our office but was not expecting a call or a visit from the senior pastor. I passed this information along, and Adam was able to connect with this family and pray with them before surgery.

Administrative assistants must be detail oriented—and related to that is being able to recall details. Many times we have been in meetings and a free flow of ideas, thoughts, and plans has been running around the table. Often plans will get made without the group having all the information. It is critical for the administrative assistant to be able to confirm dates and the availability of people and resources when plans are being formed. If you know recall of dates and other information is not one of your strengths, make sure you have the resources with you to confirm these items on the spot so that plans can either move forward or be changed as needed.

Staying five steps ahead while following

When you know the pastor's priorities and work style, you will be able to anticipate what is needed for many different situations. In this way it is important to stay ahead of your pastor in preparing for meetings, trips, and projects. If you know the pastor likes to have certain tools available during presentations, you can make sure those are ready to go.

MAKE TIME FOR THIS

One of the important things I know about my particular job and ministry situation is that the pastor doesn't like to be surprised. He likes to be fully informed regarding anything in which he is directly involved. If he is speaking somewhere, I keep him informed about who will be at the event, who is providing the introduction, and any

people at the event with whom he should connect. He likes to know if we will have visitors at
the church, who they are, why they are visiting,
and who is hosting them.

But, no surprises isn't a hard and steadfast rule. A great
example of this is the time a congregation member wanted
to surprise Adam with a special lunch. This congregation
member had me put his name on Adam's calendar as having a lunch appointment and arranged for the restaurant to
provide him with the check for the lunch. When Adam
arrived he was pleasantly surprised to find his own wife
instead of the congregation member—and had a delightful
unplanned lunch "date." This was a great blessing and a
time when a surprise was okay!

While anticipating and staying ahead of your pastor,
remember your role as the support person. Even though there
are things you can anticipate and take care of, also remember to ask what is needed and make sure the pastor is prepared for the next thing on his or her schedule.

Maintain open and honest communication

Once you know how the pastor likes to receive information, work to maintain an open communication link.

• If your pastor prefers e-mail, recap information he or she
needs to know that day and provide information about the
next day's schedule with pertinent information attached.
• For face-to-face communication, put yourself on your pastor's calendar at some point of the day.
• For communication items that are more long-range, schedule a longer meeting once a week. This time is good to go
over correspondence, provide updates for ongoing projects,
talk about future calendar items and planning, and just to
connect about information you each need to share.

It is critical to communicate honestly when you have made a mistake in your work. I am referring not to small everyday types of errors, but to those things that can and will have repercussions. I was reading the book *Managing UP* by Rosanne Badowski, former executive assistant to Jack Welch, CEO of General Electric (NY: Doubleday, 2004). I was struck by the section of her book called "The Art of Confession" in which she tells the story of a check she forgot to send to the IRS for Mr. Welch, an error that ended up costing him a few thousand dollars. While she waited to tell him about the error, he found out about the mistake when a notice was sent to his home. "Why didn't you tell me about this?" was the inevitable question. She writes, "Hiding mistakes—'moving on,' if you prefer—short-circuits the learning process that often turns a bad situation into one where some value can be salvaged" (24).

If you make a mistake, it can result in a very difficult conversation, but once you lay it out and have your discussion there is another level of trust you have reached—the level where your pastor knows you will admit your mistakes and learn from them.

Identify and work to resolve conflict

Hand-in-hand with open and honest communication is resolving any conflicts that may arise in your office. To maintain a positive atmosphere in the office, schedule a brief time to talk about issues or actions that may have caused conflict. As in any relationship, sometimes there are misunderstandings, but because you work so closely together in a sometimes emotionally charged environment, there should be no "suffering in silence."

OOPS

Several years ago, when PDAs were first intro-duced, Adam told me he was interested in using one. We talked briefly about what he needed, and I went on my way to research the different options. I visited a local electronics store and received a demonstration on all the newest PDAs on the mar-ket. I settled on one that I thought would do every-thing Adam needed. When I gave it to Adam and took him through a little demo showing him all the features, he was very gracious, but I saw a hint of disappointment on his face. I left his office know-ing I had made a mistake with the purchase and couldn't figure out how to fix it. As I was prepar-ing to leave for the day I finally just asked him to tell me if he was not happy with the PDA. Well, he wasn't happy, but he didn't want to hurt my feel-ings. We were then able to resolve the matter. Rather than let that situation be a wedge in our working relationship, it was important to ask ques-tions and get honest answers.

Handling conflict is a very important skill. A good assistant will need to be able to identify conflict and have the personal strength to go directly to the person and work together to identify resolutions to the problem. This is important in deal-ings with your senior pastor, coworkers, and congregation members.

The Effective Administrative Assistant

The American Management Association conducted a survey of administrative assistants and their managers several years ago, asking each group to name the important core competencies for an administrative assistant. It was surprising to find that each group had different ideas about what the top competencies were:

Administrative Assistants' List of Top Competencies
Initiative
Professional Demeanor
Written/Verbal Communication Skills

Managers' List of Top Competencies
Problem Solving and Decision Making Skills
Meeting and Event Management
Flexibility

(2003; www.amanet.org/research)

This report demonstrates how two people, working together, can be on two different pages. It is important to talk often with your pastor about what is expected of you in your ministry, but more important is for you to look at the types of projects your pastor is involved in and match up your pastor's needs with your skill set and gifts.

Traits

The following is a list of traits that particularly apply to ministry work to help an assistant provide the kind of support that will keep a pastor on track.

▷ **Self-starting**—Your role is to provide management for your pastor's ministry, so to be effective you can't wait to be told what to do. In order for the pastor to accomplish his or her ministry, you will need to step up to the plate, take responsibility, and move things forward. If you are waiting for the pastor to tell you what to do, you will find that many things will bottleneck in your office and lead to ineffective ministry. One caveat, however. The administrative assistant must work within the boundaries you and your pastor have set for your office. If something occurs that is outside your authority and the pastor is not available, talk with the appropriate member of the church staff.

▷ **Intuitive**—You should be able to understand the dynamics of a team and have the ability to anticipate needs. In chapter 2 I discussed the importance of learning your pastor's work style. It is also important to learn the dynamics of the pastor's team. With the executive team at The Church of the Resurrection, there are nine staff members and one volunteer providing leadership for the various ministries of the church and providing insights and counsel for Adam. Knowing the dynamics of the team helps in a number of ways, from knowing how each member likes to receive information to knowing how each organizes projects and events.

▷ **Problem Solving**—You should be able to determine priorities and have the ability to take ownership. Early in my ministry, when I would have my weekly meeting with Adam, inevitably there would be some sort of problem on the agenda that needed solving. I would present the problem to Adam and he would think about it for a few minutes. The question that always followed was, "What do you think we should do?" After the third week of receiving this question I finally got the hint that I should not just be coming in with the problem, but I should have two or three suggestions prepared for how we could handle certain issues. Sometimes he would take my suggestions, sometimes the solution might be a combination of the suggestions, and oftentimes my suggestions would be the jumping off point for a solution that Adam would craft. Pastors will appreciate this type of proactive thinking for several reasons—one, they have so much on their minds it is sometimes difficult to come up with THE solution to an issue on the spot. Two, the assistant presenting solutions from a different perspective may provide pastors with different insights; an administrative assistant's view of how things are working can be very different from pastors' viewpoints. Third, the assistant's ideas may be helpful in sparking other avenues of thought on the issue.

▷ **Self-controlled**—Working alongside a pastor can sometimes be stressful. You are often talking with people who are experiencing devastating and life-altering crisis. As the assistant and ministry manager in the office, it is critical for you to be able to present a solid, even-keeled demeanor to those with whom you are working and talking. If you are on the phone with parents who have just lost a child, the situation will spin out of control if you are not able to manage your emotions regarding the situation. What the parents need is a listening ear and a calm voice; their life is out of control and they will need to talk with someone who can provide them with stability as they work through the process of planning the next steps. For times such as these it is helpful to have someone you can turn to who is detached from these events and with whom you can sit down and unload and pray. Ask another staff member if he or she would be your support person for these types of emotional events.

Also, it can make for a stressful work environment if you let changes throw you into a tailspin. Because I know how our office works and that things often change at the last minute, I keep myself available and flexible during these times. I try not to have anything scheduled, and I prepare to run and gather needed materials as last-minute decisions are made. There are times people will say, "But we decided things were going to happen this way . . ." I just remind them we have to remain flexible. Flexibility in an assistant is a much sought-after trait that many pastors do not realize they cherish—until they have an assistant who doesn't possess this trait.

▷ **Resourceful**—Sometimes when you have lemons, your only alternative is to just make lemonade.

Practicalities

On the practical side of being an administrative assistant, you must keep current with the latest technology tools. Keep up-to-date on computer programs. Learn to use many of the features of your e-mail program. Learn how to navigate the Internet. Research websites that may be helpful in your ministry and the ministry of your church. Learn to use your county library website since it can provide you with access to thousands of periodicals and newspapers that are a great resource for sermon research.

Know the church staff. Learn who on your staff is trained to handle various situations you might encounter. Learn what constitutes an emergency and know who is the best resource for different situations—surprisingly, it might not be the senior pastor.

And while this may not be a practicality, it's so important. Know how to pray—both in person and over the phone. I have found that being a good listening ear and assuring people that you have heard them and can tell them what your next steps will be on their behalf can help calm them. When you pray with a caller before you end the conversation, you will have a person who feels well cared for and confident that he or she will receive a follow-up contact.

Resource Recommendations

I have provided a brief resource list of books and training courses that can help the administrative assistant be the effective partner in ministry to bring people to God.

Gregg's Reference Manual, 10th ed. William A. Sabin (Career Education, 2004). This is the ultimate style guide for any office.

SEND: The Essential Guide to Email for Office and Home. David Shipley and Will Schwalbe (Knopf, 2007). Writing, reading, and handling e-mail is a dilemma for many professionals today. This is a great little guide and a handy resource book.

The Microsoft Crabby Office Lady Tells It Like It Is: Secrets to Surviving Office Life. Annik Stahl (Microsoft Press, 2006).

Managing UP: How to Forge an Effective Relationship with Those Above You. Rosanne Badowski (Doubleday, 2003).

CHAPTER FOUR

Ins and Outs of the Job—and the Ministry

Often you are the first person someone will talk with regarding a need or information. When it comes to the staff and volunteers, you are the conduit for communication. The administrative assistant needs to be able to build relationships and bridges for the staff, the congregation, and the community. The staff members need to know when they talk with you—the administrative assistant—that they will be represented clearly to the pastor and they will get answers or information they need in a timely manner.

Building relationships and bridges is where great "customer service" comes in. Because you are the conduit for communication and the person who will address most of the requests that are presented, it is important that people feel welcomed and valued when they call or come to your office. Provide an environment for people to express themselves and this will go a long way in streamlining how you can care for the staff and visitors who call or enter your office.

Simple and Basic Customer Service Tips

 We need to understand who the customers are both in and outside our ministries. As assistant to a senior pastor or ministry director, you will have many customers: your coworkers, congregation members, members of the community, people who call in from other churches and businesses, and so on. While customer service is a discipline of its own in today's work world, three simple tips will help in all day-to-day dealings. These tips help me in working toward a positive experience in all of my dealings and communications—I'm sure anyone can profit by them.

1. Please and thank you language in all communication

Please and *thank you* are words we learn as children when we are asking for something and as a way of acknowledging something we have received. In day-to-day business dealings these two simple but powerful terms can make a great impact on your relationships. Whenever I am requesting something—information, a room set-up, a meeting—I try to always remember to use the term *please* first. As the "voice" for the senior pastor, the administrative assistant could easily lapse into an "authority" voice, so he or she should be sure to watch this.

I also find the word *please* can help soften something I have to tell a congregation member that may not be well received. Many e-mails are comments about a sermon or something happening in the church or the community, and people want to share the information with the senior pastor. Because we have 15,000 members and Adam receives sometimes more than 100 e-mails each day, it is impossible for him to personally respond to each one, despite the fact that he would like to do so. So, I respond to acknowledge receipt of these messages. I will mention something about the information contained in the e-mail and then follow it up with this statement, "Please know that because of the large number of messages we receive in our office each day Adam is not able to personally respond; he does however try to read each message." The use of the word *please* at the beginning of this statement shows the recipient that the message was received by someone who cares and took the time to acknowledge the communication. It also addresses in a polite and respectful manner the unspoken expectation that Adam would respond to the e-mail. A simple *please* goes a long way in communicating that a person who cares is looking at the message and forwarding it to the senior pastor. Instead of feeling brushed aside the sender feels heard.

2. Always identify yourself by name on the phone and in electronic communication

I find it very frustrating when I call people on the phone and they don't identify themselves when they answer. Being able to use someone's name is a great way to connect and starts the conversation off on a friendly and caring note. This connection will typically lead to a more friendly service-oriented conversation. Jesus always acknowledged the people he encountered and addressed them in such a way that they knew they were important and had value and were loved by God. This is a good example for us to follow.

It is also important to make this same type of acknowledgment in e-mail. When you are sending a message by e-mail that will first go through the intended recipient's assistant, acknowledge the assistant. We all have challenging ministries, and it is important to acknowledge there is a human being receiving our communication who is working to help take care of our request or need.

3. Should the answer to a request be No (period) or No (comma)?

Like in all organizations, the church has policies and procedures that need to be followed for the organization to function smoothly on a day-to-day basis. Our policies and procedures sometimes prompt us to answer No. (period) to some of the requests we receive. However, the church is a living, breathing, organic organization and we try to meet people where they are, so shouldn't our answer to requests we receive that we cannot accommodate sometimes be No, (comma)? What I mean by this is, should the response be "No, I'm sorry we can't do this; however, I can offer you this as an alternative."

A request that cannot be accommodated should be answered with: "No, but let's talk and see if there is some other way we can meet your request." A good example of this in our office is when congregation members call and ask for a counseling appointment with Adam. Because of the sheer volume of people seeking counseling appointments, an entire team of pastors and laity serve to meet the congregational care needs of our church. So when people call, I talk with them a bit about their need and work to get them connected with a pastor in the Congregational Care Office or the best person to help them with their need or concern. Occasionally someone will refuse this help and hang up the phone in frustration. When this happens it is the person who has set the answer at No. (period) and we just leave the call where it ended. If the person calls back, I will continue to work on a solution for him or her. I always try to have my answer be No, (comma) and try to work out a solution that will meet the need.

Identification of Tasks

The pastor and assistant need to look at all the tasks the pastor currently has that can be handed off to the assistant. A great place to begin this conversation is by asking your pastor to identify what things he or she is doing that prevent the ministry from being taken to the next level. What are those tasks that take up a lot of time and can be done by the administrative assistant? Transfer of tasks will not happen with one conversation; it will be a series of conversations over a number of months and sometimes years. As the assistant, you should constantly be assessing your gifts along with your pastor's priority list and be aware of the tasks that your pastor has assumed. As you see things that you can take over, have a conversation about it.

How the Basics Work in Our Office

I receive many questions about how some of the basics work in our office. The list that follows developed over time and as our partnership developed.

The calendar and scheduling

When I became Adam's assistant, he was doing his own scheduling. The first thing he asked me to do was to purchase a large Franklin Planner (this was before electronic calendars) to maintain a copy of his calendar in my office. We both would schedule appointments. Two people scheduling appointments for one person on two different calendars is a recipe for disaster—time blocks will get double-booked, appointments will be on one calendar and not the other, and meetings will be missed. It is not an efficient way to keep a schedule.

Maintaining a calendar takes time. You need to figure in prep time for meetings and presentations, juggle and move appointments for emergencies that happen, and always have an overall picture of a week or a month at a time so that the person does not become overbooked. About four months into my ministry Adam turned all of his scheduling over to me.

After that, the following procedures developed:

▷ Everything goes on the calendar: sermon writing time, appointments, meetings, phone calls, scheduled meeting meals, prep time for presentations, vacations; and many times, family commitments. Scheduling is directed by your pastor's priorities. Putting everything on the calendar will help prevent time from slipping away.

▷ Adam has his calendar electronically on his phone so that he knows what is on the horizon; however, when people ask him about scheduling appointments his response is, "Please call my assistant since she handles my calendar."

▷ We maintain Adam's calendar on Microsoft Outlook, but I still maintain a by-the-month Franklin Planner. I depend on it to look at several weeks or months in relationship to one another. If your pastor is asked to make a presentation to your local Rotary Club, he or she may be available for the specific date and time; however, prep time will be needed for that presentation and that is easy to discern when you can open a monthly calendar with everything on the schedule and see how the prep time fits into the schedule.

▷ We are careful to not have the schedule so inflexible that the pastor is never available. There must be wiggle-room in the day—an old friend may drop by, a staff member may have an emergency, a congregation member may have a crisis. During these times you need to have the flexibility built into the schedule for the pastor to be available. It is better for the pastor to be available to pray with a member in crisis for five or ten minutes and then to connect that person with another pastor or staff member who can assist him or her than for the answer to always be that the pastor is not available.

Phone calls

In our office, we discovered that most of the time when people call it isn't the senior pastor they really need to talk to—it is another staff member. But, those calls can be land mines for a relational person—chit-chat can go on for twenty minutes. And that's twenty minutes of unscheduled time. Incoming phone calls cannot be scheduled, so unless it is an emergency or a call I know Adam is waiting for, he is not available to take incoming phone calls. In a case like this, the administrative assistant should be able to answer the phone caller's question or get the person who can. In our office, if Adam needs to return the call, it goes on the calendar.

Drop-in visitors

The principles we use for incoming phone calls will also apply to drop-in visitors. I welcome them and talk with them about what they need and work to either meet their need or get them connected with the staff member who can assist them. Of course, it may be one of the exceptions noted above.

Letter writing

The administrative assistant can write much of the pastor's correspondence. To prepare for taking over the letter writing duties in your office, read as many letters as you can that your pastor has written. Pay attention to the different tones and words used. Listen to phrasing. Let your pastor know that you need corrections and guidance as you are learning to write much of the day-to-day correspondence.

E-mail

Hand-in-hand with phone calls and letter writing is e-mail. Nothing will eat up a schedule more quickly than e-mail. In some ways e-mail has made us more efficient, and in many ways it bogs us down. If the volume of e-mail messages is large

---

○ ○ ○　　　　✉ Reply to your e-mail

To: *Click here to add recipients*
Cc:

Subject:

▶ Attachments: *none*

Font ▾　Font Size ▾　B　*I*　U　T

Thank you for taking the time to e-mail our office. Please know that because of the number of messages we receive Adam is not able to personally respond. He does, however, read each message.

(Personal comment about the e-mail would be added here.)

For any questions or further assistance, please let me know.

Blessings,

Sue Thompson
Executive Assistant to the Senior Pastor
(phone number here)

---

day after day, important items can fall through the cracks. Several years ago our procedure changed so that all of the senior pastor's e-mails now go through my office. I read them and pass messages along to the appropriate staff members for them to respond to requests and provide information. Those messages that Adam needs to see personally I respond to and forward to him.

I have a standard response I use with most messages I pass along to Adam. (See opposite page.)

I then forward the e-mail and my response on to Adam.

We will receive messages that need a personal response from Adam and I send those on to him with an indication that I did not send a response. Depending on the nature of the e-mail, Adam will either send the person a response or send a response for me to forward on.

Sermon Research

Research can be very time consuming and take a lot of precious sermon preparation time. From time to time I assist Adam with his sermons by providing some of the research for his messages. I do not do the biblical or theological research, but I do provide statistical or study research pertaining to the topic on which Adam will preach. There are many tools available to help any administrative assistant become a research assistant for the pastor. One place to start is with your local county library system. Often the library system will offer training sessions for using their tools online. Another place, of course, is the Internet. If you don't use the Internet much, your local community college may offer classes on Internet research. These classes will offer great basic research techniques for finding reliable Internet information. (And do always make sure your Internet sources are reliable—there are a lot of sources that may look like valid sources but aren't.)

If the pastor plans sermons several months in advance, create a file for each sermon and begin the process of collecting research information for each sermon. Check major news websites daily, read weekly news magazines, and check your city's newspaper since all of these are solid resources for news stories and special features that may relate to certain sermons. National Public Radio and the PBS websites are also great resources.

In a Nutshell

For a quick recap of this chapter, here is a list of questions for you to think about that will help you become an effective administrative assistant.

1. What are the pastor's top priorities? Have today's priorities changed for any reason? Does the pastor's schedule reflect his or her priorities?

2. What in the pastor's work style impedes a schedule? What can you do to assist and keep projects moving forward?

3. Whom do you go to for decisions when the pastor is out of the office or unreachable?

4. Who are the people heading up each ministry area in your church? What are their responsibilities? To whom do they report? What is the contact information for each of these people?

5. Who are frequent visitors to the office—church leadership, community leaders, area pastors, friends, family? Whom does the pastor meet

46

with on a regular basis? Do you know these people's full names, where they work, their titles, contact information?

6. What is the pastor's preferred work schedule? What hours will he or she be in the office?

7. How does the pastor prefer to receive information? How does the pastor prefer to be contacted?

8. Does the pastor like to have uninterrupted quiet time in the office? Is there a place he or she likes to work away from the office? When is the most productive time to schedule meetings?

9. Do you clearly understand what constitutes an emergency for the pastor and do you know how to handle emergency interruptions? Who else on your staff (or as designated laypeople) can you turn to for handling emergencies? Do you have all the necessary emergency contact information to reach the pastor and family members? (See page 49.)

10. Which community organizations and denominational or professional groups does the pastor belong to? Are there regularly scheduled meetings for these organizations and groups? Are these standing appointments on the pastor's schedule?

11. What tasks or duties does the pastor regularly handle that you can take off his or her desk? Are there things you can do to help free up time in the pastor's schedule? Are there office procedures or certain regular tasks that the pastor

doesn't like to handle and is there a way for you to streamline a process or re-design certain tasks to make them less of a burden?

12. Personal information may be optional: frequent flyer information, health insurance information, Social Security number, name and ages of children and where they go to school or live. Be sure if you have this information that it is kept in a safe place. Are there preferences for local restaurants?

13. What type of feedback does the pastor like to receive from you?

Emergency Contact Information

Pastor's Family	Home Phone	Cell Phone
1.		
2.		
3.		
4.		
5.		
6.		

When Pastor Can't Be Reached *Ruling Elders*

Name	Ministry Area	Office Phone	Cell Phone
1.			
2.			
3.			
4.			
5.			

The Job Description

A job description is critical in laying out what your responsibilities are for your ministry. And here I'll repeat what I wrote in chapter 1: A call to ministry is an important thing for an administrative assistant to understand; your heart and the way you deal with people and tasks are different if you understand your position as a call to ministry rather than a job for a paycheck.

So, with that said, on to the job description itself. The description is meant not to be a laundry list of duties, but a guideline of what is expected of you. As an example, here is how my job description is worded:

The United Methodist Church of the Resurrection
Job Description
Executive Assistant to the Senior Pastor
Position: Full Time, Salaried   Reports to: Senior Pastor

Summary:
Organize and direct the activities of the Senior Pastor's office and provide professional skills and support for the Senior Pastor's ministry.

Qualifications:
• Desire to serve the Lord
• Confidentiality
• Flexibility

- Ability to relate to all staff and volunteers in all areas
- Ability to function as a team member and/or leader
- Strong organizational skills
- Ability to organize and direct projects from start to finish
- Self starter
- Excellent people and phone skills
- Excellent verbal and written communication skills
- Strong computer skills:
  Database, Word, Excel, Publisher, Computer Calendar, E-mail, Internet, etc.
- Strong problem solving skills

Essential Duties and Responsibilities:

The position of Executive Assistant to Senior Pastor includes, but is not limited to, the following duties:

- Maintain Senior Pastor's office
- Build and maintain strong relationships with all ministry areas
- Create a warm hospitable atmosphere for visitors in the office
- Manage the Senior Pastor's calendar
  - ✓ Coordinate the scheduling of appointments and meetings
  - ✓ Prepare daily calendar
  - ✓ Attach pertinent information to calendar for Senior Pastor to reference
  - ✓ Protect study and sermon writing time
  - ✓ Coordinate other project preparation time
- Have all information prepared for weekend worship
  - ✓ Baptisms
  - ✓ Announcements
  - ✓ COR happenings
  - ✓ Worship rundown
- Manage phone calls and correspondence
  - ✓ Answer incoming phone calls
  - ✓ Know where to direct phone calls
  - ✓ Prompt return of voice mail
  - ✓ Manage mail
  - ✓ Prepare and mail correspondence from Senior Pastor
  - ✓ Manage and respond to all e-mail
- Schedule meetings
  - ✓ Notify appropriate people
  - ✓ Secure room
  - ✓ Prepare meeting materials
  - ✓ Oversee set-up

- Create, maintain, and purge Senior Pastor's files
- Assist with projects and large events (at the Senior Pastor's direction)
  - ✓ Serve as a member of event planning teams
  - ✓ Manage details
- Assist with worship
  - ✓ Weekly worship planning meetings
  - ✓ Sermon research
- Deal with speaking requests
  - ✓ Schedule and coordinate all speaking requests
  - ✓ Organize materials for event
  - ✓ Schedule travel
  - ✓ Maintain close communications with host church/organization
- Serve as a resource for other ministry areas in relation to the Senior Pastor's ministry
- Attend weekly staff chapel, executive staff meeting, meet weekly with Senior Pastor for coordinating, planning, and communication
- Be actively involved in the life and ministry of COR
- Perform all other duties as assigned by the Senior Pastor

As with everything else in the work life of an assistant, flexibility is key. Don't let your job description confine you in what you do as a partner for your pastor, but let it be your jumping-off point to take your skills and responsibilities to the next level.

A Word to Pastors

This chapter speaks directly to the pastor, the associate pastor, ministry director or coordinator, or the team whose responsibility is leadership. If you're the administrative assistant reading this, you might want to suggest that they read it. I'll start with some advice to the leader.

Support the Administrative Assistant

The most effective administrative assistants will be rendered ineffective and powerless to assist if they do not have the support of the person for whom they work. Effective assistants make hundreds of decisions a day that will impact the ministry of the person they work for. Assistants will usually make decisions based on history and experience and take into consideration all of the things they have learned about the pastor. Effective assistants cannot make decisions in a vacuum.

If you disagree with a decision the administrative assistant has made or an answer given to someone, it is important that you talk with your assistant about how and why that decision was made. Just as it is important for an assistant not to disagree with the pastor in public, the same applies to the pastor with the assistant. If you think a decision needs to be reversed, talk with your assistant about the situation and how it can be resolved. Once you have cut the legs out from under your assistant to a person or a group, it will be difficult for your assistant to act in your behalf in the future.

One important way to support your assistant is to talk about and hold up the assistant's role to the congregation. For example, occasionally Adam will talk about something I have done to help prepare him for a sermon or a presentation. It will help your assistant in dealings with congregation members if the congregation knows about the assistant and the many things the assistant does not only for you but also to support the ministries of the church and its members. If your staff and congregation understand that this is the person you trust to walk alongside you in your ministry, they also will trust your assistant to work with them on your behalf, freeing you up to concentrate on those things that only you can do.

Encourage

There are days that being an assistant can be a very unpleasant position. People might be rude and they might be disrespectful. There will be days when your assistant will talk with people who have just experienced a terrible loss and be emotionally devastated. An effective assistant will respond with grace even when the situation is difficult. Just as a pastor can experience an emotional overload so can the assistant. These situations can build up into frustration and burnout over time, and a person can begin to feel as though he or she is not doing a good job. Recognize that there will be times that assistants will need to hear they are doing a great job and that they are appreciated. If you hear a story about how your assistant had a positive impact on someone, share that story with the assistant: we all need things in our "feel good" file that we can pull out on those tough days.

I heard a story about a pastor who at the end of each Friday turns to his assistant before he leaves for the day and says, "It was a pleasure to serve Christ here with you this week." That's encouragement.

Communicate

I can't say enough about communication. Effective communication will take a mediocre pastor/assistant work relationship and turn it into a dynamic duo relationship. The most effective assistant is one who knows what is happening, what is expected, what is needed, and what the goals are. An assistant shouldn't have to guess about these things. Pastors, include your assistants in important meetings so they will hear firsthand your responsibilities, goals, and expectations. Details should be provided for the assistant when attendance at the meeting isn't possible.

As an assistant it can be embarrassing to get a phone call asking about an important project involving the pastor and to have to admit that you have no information. Lack of communication can slow down progress or cause the administrative assistant to feel ineffective.

Invest

Just as other professionals attend continuing education events or conferences to recharge their batteries and refresh and renew their skills, administrative assistants need the same opportunities. A small investment in continuing education for the administrative assistant can provide great benefits for the church. Is there a new computer program that would help improve the administration or a ministry area? Send the administrative assistant and have him or her bring back the information and train the rest of the staff. Are there new and innovative office management systems that would benefit the church? Send the assistant to learn some new and improved ways of office management to implement in the church office. With a little training could your assistant help manage projects in your church? There are inexpensive management workshops for administrative assistants that could provide basic project management skills.

Providing training opportunities will provide many benefits for your church and will also serve as a source of encouragement—it shows your willingness to move outside the box, so to speak, to discover what this partner in ministry can do to help develop and grow your church.

Provide Feedback

Timely feedback is critical at all times but especially when an administrative assistant is learning a new job and new responsibilities. I would even refer to this as coaching. When something doesn't meet expectations, it is best to sit down at the earliest possible time and talk about where a project has fallen short and the impact it had on the ministry or a certain outcome. It is much more productive to address issues while they are fresh in everyone's mind. Addressing issues when they occur also helps prevent resentment from building for all parties concerned. When timely feedback is provided, the administrative assistant can work to develop possible solutions and reduce the possibility of a disappointment the next time the situation occurs.

Trust and Be Confident

Since pastors are often away from their office, trust and confidence are important. When pastors have taken the time to build a good solid working relationship with their assistants, have had the necessary conversations about expectations, and equipped assistants with information and the tools needed, they then need to show trust and confidence in the assistants' abilities. Trust and confidence start with the small things and soon pastors will find their ministry can expand because they trust their assistants to manage the day-to-day details.

Listen to and Value Input

Recognize that the administrative assistant will have a unique and sometimes different perspective on many things that are happening in your church—people often will say things to your assistant that they might not say to you. Your administrative assistant can be a resource with a different take on things that can be a great benefit to your ministry.

Your assistant might see ways to streamline and enhance your ministry and improve customer service in your church. If the environment in your church office is open and the administrative assistant feels encouraged to share ideas, you may find that these ideas will be a blessing to you and to your congregation.

Ask: "Is Anything Needed?"

On any given day, the administrative assistant learns of about a dozen things that the pastor needs. I would encourage you as the pastor to occasionally ask your assistant if anything is needed. There might be particular areas the assistant would like to strengthen through a class or retreat time, maybe its something for the office, maybe other things. But ask . . .

Conclusion

As I wrote in the introduction that an important part of the administrative assistant's job is to pray for the pastor daily, assistants will be encouraged daily when they know they are included in the pastor's prayers.